THE TOWER AIR FRYER COOKBOOK UK

(WITH COLOR PICTURES)

1000 DAYS OF QUICK, EASY AND DELICIOUS TRADITIONAL ENGLISH RECIPES FOR BEGINNERS AND PROS. TIPS AND TRICKS FOR PERFECT USING

[Daphne White]

INTRODUCTION

If you are looking for a healthier way to cook your food, then you need to get yourself a tower air fryer. This cooking appliance is taking the world by storm because it uses little to no oil to cook food. That means you can enjoy all your favourite fried foods without all the unhealthy fats and oils.

The tower air fryer cookbook will show you how to make delicious and healthy meals with your air fryer. You will be amazed at all the different things you can make with this little appliance. From French fries to chicken wings, there is nothing that you cannot make in an air fryer.

This cookbook includes over 100 recipes designed in an air fryer. Each recipe includes detailed instructions and full-colour photos to easily follow along. The bulk of the book is dedicated to recipes, divided into sections for breakfast, lunch, dinner, and dessert. Recipes include classic air fryer dishes and more creative fare, such as air-fried bananas. You will also find tips and tricks for getting the most out of your air fryer.

So, what are you waiting for? Get your hands on the tower air fryer cookbook today and start cooking healthier meals for you and your family.

Getting to know the tower air fryer

The tower air fryer is one of the most popular kitchen appliances in the market today. This high-tech cooking device is loved by home cooks and chefs alike for its ability to produce delicious, crispy fried foods without all the unhealthy fats and oils typically found in traditional frying methods.

But how exactly does this amazing appliance work? The tower air fryer uses a combination of super-hot air and rapid spinning to cook your food. The hot air quickly cooks the outer layers of your food, while the fast-spinning ensures that all sides are evenly cooked and crispy.

In addition to its superior frying capabilities, the tower air fryer also has many other benefits. It is much more energy-efficient than traditional frying methods, making it a great choice for those looking to reduce their environmental impact.

Furthermore, the tower air fryer is extremely easy to use and requires very little maintenance. With just a few simple steps, you can whip up delicious fried foods any time you want! So, if you're looking for an efficient, convenient, and healthy way to prepare your favourite fried foods, the tower air fryer is your best bet!

How does tower air fryer works?

The tower air fryer works by circulating hot air around the food at high speeds, cooking it quickly and evenly. This allows you to achieve crispy, golden-brown results without using any oil or other unhealthy fats. The tower air fryer's advanced heating technology also helps retain more nutrients in your food than traditional frying methods, making it a healthier choice for your family.

The tower air fryer is also very easy to use, with simple temperature and time controls that allow you to customize your cooking experience. So, whether you are cooking a quick snack or preparing a big meal, the tower air fryer is the perfect tool for all your frying needs.

The benefits of the tower air fryer

The tower air fryer is a great choice for anyone looking to enjoy fried foods without the health risks associated with traditional frying methods. Some of the many benefits of using a tower air fryer include:

1. **Air frying is safer and healthier than deep frying.**

Air-fried food is a healthier alternative to deep-frying. They have lower fat and calories than traditional fried foods. An air fryer is a great option if you are looking to lose weight, reduce your fat intake, or modify or cut down on fried foods.

2. **Air fryers save time.**

An air fryer can cook a chicken breast much faster than an oven. They cook food faster because they are smaller than ovens and circulate air with fans.

3. **Versatility**

Air fryers can also be used to bake, grill, and roast. It fries much better than an oven. It can also bake (even cakes), roast, broil, grill, and stir fry!

4. **Easy to clean**

The most tedious part of cooking is cleaning up. An air fryer is easy to clean. Non-stick coating parts ensure that food doesn't stick to the pan. After use, it takes only a few minutes for you to clean up.

5. **Ideal for picky eaters**

Air-frying can also be a great option for those who are picky about vegetables. The vegetable can easily be crisped up using the air fryer to make it tastier.

Tips and tricks on how to use the tower air fryer

There are various tips that can help you get the best out of your tower air fryer.

1. Start by preheating your tower air fryer to the desired temperature. This may take a few minutes, depending on the size and power of your unit.

2. Add small or thin pieces of food first, such as chicken tenders or French fries. These items will cook more quickly than larger or thicker pieces of food, so they are a good place to start when learning how to use your tower air fryer effectively.

3. Keep an eye on your food while it is cooking in order to avoid burning or overcooking it. Using tongs can help you easily flip and remove foods from the pan without getting burned!

4. To get perfectly crispy results with minimal oil or fat every time, use a cooking spray or brush to lightly coat the pan before adding your food.

5. Make sure your air fryer parts are completely dry before storing them. Leaving wet parts in the unit can lead to rusting and other damage over time, so always ensure everything is clean and dry before putting it away.

Cleaning and maintenance of the tower air fryer

Tower Air fryers can be cleaned and maintained easily, thanks to the non-stick coating on most frying pans. These tips will help you keep your air fryers in top condition.

Before cleaning your tower air fryer, always unplug it and allow it to cool completely.

1. Baked on foods: Apply a mixture made of baking soda and water over the area affected. Use a bristle brush to clean the area. Finally, wipe it clean with a bristle brush or a paper towel.

2. To remove difficult-to-reach food items, soak the frying pan or basket in hot water and then rinse with dishwashing detergent. Then wash them regularly or put them in the dishwasher.

3. Do not use abrasive cleaners to clean your frying pan or basket to preserve the non-stick coating. For cleaning, you can use a sponge or bristle brush.

4. Mix some vinegar and enough hot water to remove grease. After that, soak the basket and frying pan for a few moments before washing.

5. Use a damp cloth to wipe the base of your air fryer. Use a microfiber or similar cloth to clean the air fryer base.

6. After each use, remember to clean your air fryer.

7. When removing food from the frying pan, use wooden or silicone-tipped forks and utensils.

8. Make sure all removable parts are completely dried before storing.

BREAKFAST RECIPES

Tasty Baked Eggs

Preparation time: 10 min
Cooking time: 20 min
Servings: 4
Ingredients:
- 4 eggs
- 500g baby spinach
- 200g chopped ham
- 4 tablespoons milk
- 1 tablespoon olive oil
- Cooking spray
- To the taste, add salt and black pepper

Directions:
1. Place the oil in a saucepan over medium heat. Add the baby spinach and stir fry for about a minute before removing from heat.
2. Use cooking spray to grease 4 baking dishes and place baby spinach and ham into each one.
3. Crack an egg in each baking dish, add the milk, and season with salt and pepper.
4. Bake for 20 mins in a preheated oven at 175° C.
5. Serve baked eggs for breakfast. Enjoy!

Nutrition: Calories 320, fat 5g, fibre 10g, carbs 16g, protein 10g

Delicious Potato Frittata

Preparation time: 10 minutes
Cooking time: 20 minutes
Servings: 6
Ingredients:
- 16 potato wedges
- 170g of jarred roasted red bell peppers, chopped
- 12 eggs, whisked
- 50g parmesan, grated
- 3 garlic cloves, minced
- 2 tablespoons parsley, chopped
- Salt and black pepper to the taste
- 2 tablespoons chives, chopped
- 6 tablespoons ricotta cheese
- Cooking spray

Directions:
1. Combine eggs, red peppers and garlic with parsley and salt in a bowl
2. Place half the potato wedges in the bottom of the dish and then sprinkle half the parmesan on top.
3. Add half of the egg mix, and add the remaining potatoes and the parmesan.
4. Add the remaining eggs, mix, sprinkle chives.
5. Heat up your air fryer at 150°C and grease it with cooking spray.
6. Place in air fryer for 20 minutes.
7. Divide among plates and serve for breakfast.

Nutrition: Calories 310, fat 5, fibre 10, carbs 15g, protein 7g

Sausage, Eggs and Cheese Mix

Preparation time: 10 minutes
Cooking time: 22 minutes
Servings: 3
Ingredients:

- 280g sausages, cooked and crumbled
- 220g cheddar cheese, shredded
- 220g mozzarella cheese, shredded 8 eggs, whisked
- 250 ml milk
- Salt and black pepper to the taste
- Cooking spray

Directions:

1. Mix sausages, eggs, cheese, mozzarella, milk, salt, and pepper in a bowl and whisk well.
2. Place eggs and sausage mix in the air fryer.
3. Heat your air fryer at 190 degrees C.
4. Spray with cooking oil.
5. Air fry for 22 minutes.
6. Divide among plates and serve. Enjoy!

Nutrition: calories 315, fat 5, fibre 10, carbs 10, protein 7

Polenta Bites

Preparation time: 10 minutes
Cooking time: 20 minutes
Servings: 4
Ingredients:
For the polenta:

- 1 tablespoon butter
- 200g cornmeal
- 220ml water
- Salt and black pepper to the taste

For the polenta bites:

- 2 tablespoons powdered sugar
- Cooking spray

Directions:

1. Combine water, cornmeal, butter, and salt in a saucepan. Stir, then bring to a boil on medium heat. After 10 minutes, remove from heat and let cool in the refrigerator.
2. Take 1 tablespoon of polenta and shape it into a ball.
3. Repeat with the rest of the polenta, arrange all the balls in the cooking basket of your air fryer, spray them with cooking spray, cover and cook at 190°C for 8 minutes.
4. Arrange the finished polenta bites on tray, sprinkle some sugar all over.
5. Serve for breakfast.

Nutrition: Calories 225, fat 8, fibre 6, carbs 10, protein 5

Tomato and Bacon Breakfast

Preparation time: 12 minutes
Cooking time: 28 minutes
Servings: 5

ùIngredients:

- 750g canned tomatoes, chopped
- 500g white bread, cubed
- 500g smoked bacon, cooked and chopped
- ¼ cup olive oil

- 8 eggs, whisked
- 1 yellow onion, chopped
- ½ teaspoon red pepper, crushed
- 220g cheddar, shredded
- 2 tablespoons chives, chopped
- Salt and black pepper to the taste
- 200g Monterey Jack, shredded
- 2 tablespoons stock

Directions:
1. Add the bread, tomatoes, bacon, red pepper, onion, and stock in a bowl and stir.
2. Add the cheddar, eggs, and Monterey jack
3. Add the oil to the air fryer and heat it at 170 degrees C.
4. Place the mixture in the air fryer and fry for 28 minutes.
5. Divide among plates, sprinkle chives, and serve. Enjoy!

Nutrition: Calories 230, fat 6g, fibre 6g, carbs 10g, protein 5g

Breakfast Bread Pudding

Preparation time: 12 minutes
Cooking time: 26 minutes
Servings: 4
Ingredients:
- 220g white bread, cubed
- 170ml of milk
- 2 teaspoons of cornstarch
- 5 tablespoons of honey
- 1 teaspoon of vanilla extract
- 2 teaspoons of cinnamon powder 1 and 1/3 cup flour
- 120g of brown sugar
- 80g of soft butter

- 80g of apple, peeled, cored, and roughly chopped
- 170ml of water

Directions:
1. Combine bread, apple, milk, water, honey, and cinnamon in a bowl. Mix well.
2. Combine flour, sugar, and butter in a separate bowl. Stir until you get a crumbly mixture.
3. Spread half the crumble mixture on the bottom of an air fryer. Add bread and apple mix. Cook for 25 minutes at 170°C.
4. Divide the bread pudding and place it on plates. Enjoy!

Nutrition: Calories 260, fat 6g, fibre 6g, carbs 7g, protein 4g

Swiss Chard and Sausage

Preparation time: 10 minutes
Cooking time: 25 minutes
Servings: 10
Ingredients:
- 25g of mozzarella, shredded
- 1kg of Swiss chard, chopped
- 500g of sausage, chopped
- 30g of onion, chopped
- 1 tablespoon olive oil
- 25g of parmesan, grated
- 1 garlic clove, minced
- Salt and black pepper
- 3 eggs
- 500g of ricotta cheese
- A pinch of nutmeg

Directions:
1. Heat up a pan that fits your air fryer with the oil over medium heat, add onions, garlic, Swiss chard, salt, pepper, and nutmeg, stir, cook for 2 minutes and take off heat.
2. In a bowl, whisk eggs with mozzarella, parmesan and ricotta, stir, pour over Swiss chard mix, toss, introduce in your air fryer and cook at 160°C for 20 minutes.

3. Divide among plates and serve.

Nutrition: calories 330, fat 12g, fibre 3g, carbs 16g, protein 23g

Shrimp Frittata

Preparation time: 10 minutes
Cooking time: 10 minutes
Servings: 4
Ingredients:
- 4 eggs
- ½ teaspoon of basil, dried
- Cooking spray
- Salt and black pepper to the taste
- 100g of rice, cooked
- 50g of shrimp, cooked, peeled, deveined, and chopped
- 15g of baby spinach, chopped
- 80g of Monterey Jack cheese, grated

Directions:
1. Combine eggs with salt, pepper, and basil in a bowl. Mix well.
2. Spray your pan with cooking spray, then add the rice, shrimp, and spinach to your air fryer.
3. Mix eggs and cheese, then heat in an air fryer at 170°C for 10 minutes.
4. Divide on plates and enjoy your breakfast. Enjoy!

Nutrition: Calories 160, fat 5g, fibre 6g, carbs 10g, protein 5g

Raspberry Rolls

Preparation time: 35 minutes
Cooking time: 30 minutes
Servings: 6

Ingredients:
- 220ml of milk
- 4 tablespoons butter
- 150g of flour
- 2 teaspoons of yeast
- 50g of sugar
- 1 egg

For the filling:
- 225g of cream cheese, soft
- 1 teaspoon vanilla extract
- 340g of raspberries
- Zest from 1 lemon, grated
- 5 tablespoons sugar
- 1 tablespoon cornstarch

Directions:
1. Combine flour, sugar, and yeast in a bowl. Stir.
2. Combine milk and eggs, mix until you get a dough. Leave it to rise for 26 mins, then transfer the dough into a flat surface and roll it well.
3. Combine cream cheese, sugar, vanilla, and lemon zest in bowl. Stir well before spreading over dough.
4. Mix raspberries and cornstarch in a bowl. Stir, then spread the mixture over cream cheese.
5. Make your dough and cut it into small pieces. Then, heat your air fryer to dry them.

6. Spray them with cooking spray and bake for 30 minutes at 180° C.
7. Serve for breakfast. Enjoy!

Nutrition: Calories 250, fat 5g, fibre 10g, carbs 10g, protein 5g

Breakfast Broccoli Quiche

Preparation time: 12 minutes
Cooking time: 22 minutes
Servings: 3
Ingredients:
- 1 teaspoon of thyme
- 3 carrots, chopped and steamed
- 50g of cheddar cheese, grated
- 2 eggs
- 60ml of milk
- 1 tomato, chopped
- 1 teaspoon of parsley, chopped
- Salt and black pepper to the taste
- 1 broccoli head, florets separated and steamed

Directions:
1. Combine eggs, milk, parsley, and thyme in a saucepan. Stir well.
2. In your air fryer pan, place broccoli, carrots, and tomato.
3. Spread cheddar cheese on top.
4. For 22 minutes, heat at 170°C.
5. Divide the plates among yourself and enjoy your breakfast. Enjoy!

Nutrition: Calories 215, fat 5g, fibre 8g, carbs 10g, protein 4g

Breakfast Egg Bowls

Preparation time: 11 minutes
Cooking time: 15 minutes
Servings: 5
Ingredients:
- Black pepper and Salt
- 3 tablespoons mixed parsley and chives
- 5 dinner rolls
- 5 tablespoons heavy cream
- 4 eggs
- 5 tablespoons parmesan, grated

Directions:
1. Place dinner rolls on a baking tray and crack an egg into each one.
2. Mix the heavy cream with the prepared herbs in each roll, and season with pepper and salt.
3. Spread parmesan cheese on your rolls and place them in an air fryer. Heat at 180°C for 15 minutes.
4. Place your bread on plates and enjoy breakfast!

Nutrition: Calories 240, fat 5g, fibre 6g, carbs 15g, protein 8g

Breakfast Pea Tortilla

Preparation time: 10 minutes
Cooking time: 7 minutes
Servings: 8
Ingredients:

- 220g of baby peas
- 4 tablespoons butter
- 400g of yogurt
- 8 eggs
- 15g of mint, chopped
- Salt and black pepper to the taste

Directions:

1. Heat the butter in a saucepan. Add peas and stir.
2. In the meantime, combine half the yogurt with salt, pepper, and eggs in a bowl. Mix well.
3. Mix the ingredients, then toss with the peas. Heat in an air fryer for 7 minutes at 180°C.
4. Spread the remaining yogurt on your tortilla. Slice and serve. Enjoy!

Nutrition: Calories 190, fat 6g, fibre 5g, carbs 4g, protein 6g

POULTRY RECIPES

Chicken Parmesan

Preparation time: 10 minutes
Cooking time: 10 minutes
Servings: 8
Ingredients:

- 200g of breadcrumbs
- 250g of white flour
- 3 tablespoons basil, chopped
- 20g of parmesan, grated
- 500g of chicken cutlets, skinless and boneless
- ½ teaspoon of garlic powder
- 1 egg, whisked
- Salt and black pepper to the taste
- 230g of mozzarella, grated
- 450g of tomato sauce

Directions:

1. Combine breadcrumbs, garlic powder, and parmesan in a bowl. Stir.
2. Combine flour and egg in two different bowls.
3. Season the chicken with salt, pepper, and dip in the prepare flour, egg mixture, and breadcrumbs.
4. Place chicken pieces in an air fryer. Heat the chicken for 3 minutes on each side at 190°.
5. Place the chicken in a baking dish that is large enough to fit your air fryer. Add tomato sauce and mozzarella. Finally, place

it in your air frying pan and heat it at 190°C for 7 minutes.
6. Divide on plates and sprinkle basil on top.

Nutrition: Calories 301, fat 10g, fibre 12g, carbs 20g, protein 15g

Chicken and Peaches

Preparation time: 12 minutes
Cooking time: 35 minutes
Servings: 6
Ingredients:

- 1 full chicken, cut into medium pieces
- 200ml of water
- 30ml of honey
- Salt and pepper to the taste
- 60ml of olive oil
- 4 peaches, halved

Directions:

1. Put the water in a pot, allow to simmer over medium heat, add honey, whisk until even and leave aside.
2. Rub the chicken pieces with the oil, add salt and pepper, place into the air fryer's basket and cook at 180°C for 10 minutes.
3. Brush the chicken with some honey mix, cook for about 6 minutes more, flip again, brush again with the honey mix and cook for 7 minutes more.
4. Divide chicken pieces on plates and keep warm.
5. Brush peaches with what's left of the honey marinade, place them in your air fryer, and cook them for 3 minutes.

6. Divide among plates next to chicken pieces and serve.

Nutrition: Calories 430, fat 15g, fibre 5g, carbs 12g, protein 20g

Chicken and Spinach Salad

Preparation time: 10 minutes
Cooking time: 13 minutes
Servings: 2
Ingredients:
- 1 avocado, pitted, peeled, and chopped
- ½ teaspoon of onion powder
- 2 teaspoons of sweet paprika
- 2 chicken breasts, skinless and boneless
- 120ml of lemon juice
- 150g of baby spinach
- 1 small red onion, sliced
- Salt and black pepper to the taste
- 60ml of cup olive oil
- 8 strawberries, sliced
- 2 tablespoons of balsamic vinegar
- 1 tablespoon of tarragon, chopped
- 1 teaspoon of parsley, dried

Directions:
1. Put chicken in a bowl, add lemon juice, parsley, onion powder, paprika, and toss.
2. Transfer the chicken to the tower air fryer and cook at 180°C for 13 minutes.
3. Mix spinach, onion, strawberries, and avocado in a bowl and toss.
4. Mix oil with vinegar, salt, pepper, and tarragon in another bowl, whisk well, add to the salad, and toss.

5. Divide chicken on plates, add spinach salad on the side, and serve. Enjoy!

Nutrition: Calories 240, fat 6g, fibre 14g, carbs 20g, protein 20g

Easy Duck Breasts

Preparation time: 10 minutes
Cooking time: 40 minutes
Servings: 6
Ingredients:
- 6 duck breasts, halved
- Salt and black pepper to the taste
- 3 tablespoons flour
- 6 tablespoons of butter, melted
- 500ml of chicken stock
- 120ml of white wine
- 15g of parsley, chopped
- 180g of mushrooms, chopped

Directions:
1. Season duck breasts with salt and pepper, place them in a bowl, add melted butter, toss and transfer to another bowl.
2. Combine melted butter with flour, wine, salt, pepper, and chicken stock and stir well.
3. Arrange duck breasts in a baking dish that fits your air fryer, pour the sauce over them, add parsley and mushrooms, place in your air fryer, and cook at 180°C for 40 minutes.
4. Divide among plates and serve.

Nutrition: Calories 320, fat 30g, fibre 12g, carbs 10g, protein 45g

Chicken Breasts and BBQ Chili Sauce

Preparation time: 10 minutes
Cooking time: 20 minutes
Servings: 6

Ingredients:
- 250g of chili sauce
- 450g of ketchup
- 230ml of pear jelly
- 60ml of honey
- ½ teaspoon of liquid smoke
- 1 teaspoon of chili powder
- 1 teaspoon of mustard powder
- 1 teaspoon of sweet paprika
- Salt and black pepper to the taste
- 1 teaspoon of garlic powder
- 6 chicken breasts, skinless and boneless

Directions:
1. Season chicken breasts with salt and pepper.
2. Put in the preheated air fryer and cook at 180°C for 10 minutes.
3. Meanwhile, heat a pan with the chili sauce over medium heat. Add ketchup, pear jelly, honey, liquid smoke, chili powder, mustard powder, sweet paprika, salt, pepper, and garlic powder, stir, bring to a simmer and cook in air fryer for 10 minutes.
4. Add air-fried chicken breasts, toss well, divide among plates and serve. Enjoy!

Nutrition: Calories 473, fat 15g, fibre 8g, carbs 37g, protein 30g

Turkey, Peas and Mushrooms Casserole

Preparation time: 10 minutes
Cooking time: 20 minutes
Servings: 4

Ingredients:
- 1kg of turkey breasts, skinless, boneless
- Salt and black pepper to the taste
- 1 yellow onion, chopped
- 1 celery stalk, chopped
- 70g of peas
- 230ml of chicken stock
- 240ml of cream mushrooms soup
- 70g of bread cubes

Directions:
1. In a large pan, combine turkey, salt, pepper, onion, pea, stock, and celery. Heat in your air fryer for 15 minutes at 180°C.
2. Mix bread cubes with cream of mushroom soup. Stir, toss, and cook for 5 minutes at 180°C.
3. Divide on several plates and serve hot. Enjoy!

Nutrition: Calories 270, fat 10g, fibre 10g, carbs 15g, protein 6g

Pepperoni Chicken

Preparation time: 10 minutes
Cooking time: 20 minutes
Servings: 6
Ingredients:
- Salt and black pepper to the taste
- 400ml of ounces tomato paste
- 1 tablespoon olive oil
- 1 teaspoon oregano, dried
- 170g of mozzarella, sliced
- 1 teaspoon garlic powder
- 4 medium chicken breasts, skinless and boneless
- 50g of pepperoni, sliced

Directions:
1. Mix chicken with salt, pepper, garlic powder, and oregano in a bowl and toss.
2. Put chicken in your air fryer, cook at 175°C for 5 minutes and transfer to a pan that fits your air fryer.
3. Add mozzarella slices on top, spread tomato paste, top with pepperoni slices, introduce in your air fryer and cook at 175°C for 15 minutes more.
4. Divide among plates and serve.

Nutrition: Calories 315, fat 8g, fibre 15g, carbs 20g, protein 25g

Duck and Plum Sauce

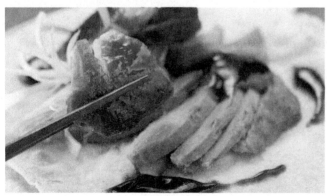

Preparation time: 10 minutes
Cooking time: 32 minutes
Servings: 2
Ingredients:
- 2 duck breasts

- 1 tablespoon butter, melted
- 1 star anise
- 1 tablespoon olive oil
- 1 shallot, chopped
- 250g of red plumps, stoned, cut into small wedges
- 2 tablespoons sugar
- 2 tablespoons red wine
- 230ml of beef stock

Directions:
1. Heat a pan with the olive oil on medium heat, add shallot, stir and cook for 5 minutes,
2. Add sugar and plums, stir and cook until sugar dissolves.
3. Add stock and wine, stir, cook for 15 minutes, take off heat and keep warm for now.
4. Prepare duck breasts, season with salt and pepper, rub with melted butter, transfer to a heat proof dish that fits your air fryer, add star anise and plum sauce, place in your air fryer and cook at 180°C for 12 minutes.
5. Divide everything on plates and serve.

Nutrition: Calories 38, fat 20g, fibre 15g, carbs 30g, protein 40g

Creamy Coconut Chicken

Preparation time: 2 hours
Cooking time: 25 minutes
Servings: 4
Ingredients:
- 4 tablespoons coconut cream
- Salt and black pepper to the taste

- 5 teaspoons turmeric powder
- 2 tablespoons ginger, grated
- 4 big chicken legs

Directions:

1. Combine cream with ginger, turmeric, salt, and pepper in a bowl. Next, whisk in coconut cream. Finally, add chicken pieces. Mix well. Leave aside for 2 hours.
2. Place the chicken in a preheated air fryer for 25 minutes at 185°C.
3. Serve alongside a side salad.

Nutrition: Calories 310, fat 5g, fibre 10g, carbs 20g, protein 18g

Chicken Salad

Preparation time: 10 minutes
Cooking time: 10 minutes
Servings: 4
Ingredients:

- 500g pound chicken breast, boneless, skinless, and halved
- Cooking spray
- Salt and black pepper to the taste
- 200g of feta cheese, cubed
- 2 tablespoons lemon juice
- 1 and ½ teaspoons mustard
- 1 tablespoon olive oil
- 1 and ½ teaspoons red wine vinegar
- ½ teaspoon anchovies, minced
- ¾ teaspoon garlic, minced
- 1 tablespoon water
- 110g of lettuce leaves, cut into strips
- 4 tablespoons parmesan, grated

Directions:

1. Spray chicken breasts with cooking oil, season with salt and pepper, introduce in your air fryer's basket, and cook at 190°C for 10 minutes, flipping halfway.
2. Transfer the chicken breasts into a cutting board, shred using 2 forks, put in a salad bowl, and mix with lettuce leaves.
3. Mix feta cheese with lemon juice, olive oil, mustard, vinegar, garlic, anchovies, water, and half of the parmesan and blend very well in your blender.
4. Add this over the chicken mix, toss, sprinkle the rest of the parmesan, and serve.

Nutrition: Calories 302, fat 5g, fibre 15g, carbs 20g, protein 25g

Quick Creamy Chicken Casserole

Preparation time: 12 minutes
Cooking time: 15 minutes
Servings: 6
Ingredients:

- 280g of spinach, chopped
- 4 tablespoons butter
- 3 tablespoons flour
- 350ml of cups milk
- 50g of parmesan, grated
- 120ml of heavy cream
- Salt and black pepper to the taste
- 300g of chicken breasts, boneless
- 120g of breadcrumbs

Directions:

1. Heat a saucepan with the butter over medium heat, add flour and stir well.

2. Add milk, heavy cream, and parmesan, stir well, cook for 1-2 minutes more and take off the heat.
3. In a pan that fits the tower air fryer, spread chicken and spinach.
4. Add salt and pepper and toss.
5. Add cream mixture and spread, sprinkle breadcrumbs on top, introduce in your air fryer and cook at 180°C for 12 minutes.
6. Divide chicken and spinach mix on plates and serve. Enjoy!

Nutrition: Calories 320, fat 10g, fibre 10g, carbs 20g, protein 15g

BEEF, PORK AND LAMB RECIPES

Garlic and Bell Pepper Beef

Preparation time: 25 minutes
Cooking time: 15 minutes
Servings: 6
Ingredients:
- 300g of steak fillets, sliced
- 2 teaspoons corn flour
- 4 garlic cloves, minced
- 2 tablespoons of olive oil
- 2 tablespoons of fish sauce
- 1 red bell pepper, cut into strips
- Black pepper to the taste
- 1 tablespoon of sugar
- 100ml beef stock
- 4 green onions, sliced

Directions:
1. Combine beef, oil, garlic, black pepper, and bell pepper in an oven-safe pan. Stir, cover, and chill in the refrigerator for 30 minutes.
2. Heat the oil in an air fryer to 180° C.
3. Combine sugar and fish sauce in a bowl. Stir well. Pour over beef and cook for 7 minutes at 180°C.
4. Mix stock with corn flour, green onions, and salt. Toss in and continue cooking at 180°C for 7 more minutes.
5. Divide on plates and serve.

Nutrition: Calories 340, fat 5g, fibre 10g, carbs 25g, protein 35g

Lamb Roast and Potatoes

Preparation time: 15 minutes
Cooking time: 45 minutes
Servings: 5
Ingredients:
- 2kg lamb roast
- 1 spring rosemary
- 3 garlic cloves, minced
- 6 potatoes, halved
- 100ml of lamb stock
- 4 bay leaves
- Salt and black pepper to the taste

Directions:
1. Place potatoes in a dish that will fit your air fryer. Add lamb, garlic, rosemary spring and salt. Toss and then place in your air fryer. Cook at 185°C for 45 minutes.
2. Slice the lamb and place on plates.

Nutrition: Calories 274g, fat 5g, fibre 10g, carbs 22g, protein 25g

Ham and Veggie Air Fried Mix

Preparation time: 15 minutes
Cooking time: 25 minutes
Servings: 5
Ingredients:
- 60g of butter
- 40g of flour
- 700ml of milk
- ½ teaspoon thyme, dried
- 400g of ham, chopped
- 170g of sweet peas
- 115g of mushrooms, halved

- 128g of baby carrots

Directions:
1. Heat a large pan that fits your air fryer with the butter over medium heat, melt it, add flour and whisk well.
2. Add milk and whisk well again and take off the heat.
3. Add thyme, ham, peas, mushrooms, and baby carrots, stir and put in the air fryer, and cook at 180°C for 20 minutes.
4. Divide everything on plates and serve. Enjoy!

Nutrition: Calories 310, fat 8g, fibre 10g, carbs 10g, protein 8g

Burgundy Beef Mix

Preparation time: 15 minutes
Cooking time: 1 hour
Servings: 6
Ingredients:
- 1kg of beef chuck roast, cubed
- 450g of canned tomatoes, chopped
- 4 carrots, chopped
- Salt and black pepper to the taste
- 15g of mushrooms, sliced
- 2 celery ribs, chopped
- 2 yellow onions, chopped
- 25ml of beef stock
- 1 tablespoon thyme, chopped
- ½ teaspoon mustard powder
- 3 tablespoons almond flour
- 230ml of water

Directions:

1. Heat an oven-safe pot that can fit your air fryer on medium heat. Add the beef and stir.
2. Stir in tomatoes, mushrooms and onions.
3. Mix water and flour in a bowl. Stir well. Add this to a pot. Toss. Heat your air fryer at 150°C for one hour.
4. Divide on plates and serve.

Nutrition: Calories 270, fat 15g, fibre 5g, carbs 15g, protein 28g

Air Fried Sausage and Mushrooms

Preparation time: 15 minutes
Cooking time: 40 minutes
Servings: 4
Ingredients:
- 3 red bell peppers, chopped
- 1kg of pork sausage, sliced
- salt and black pepper to the taste
- 1kg of Portobello mushrooms, sliced
- 2 sweet onions, chopped
- 1 tablespoon of brown sugar
- 1 teaspoon of olive oil

Directions:
1. In a baking pan that fits the air fryer, mix sausage slices with oil, mushrooms, salt, pepper, bell pepper, onion, and sugar, stir together, place in the tower air fryer and cook at 150°C for 40 minutes.
2. Place on plates and serve right away.

Nutrition: Calories 135, fat 10g, fibre 3g, carbs 10g, protein 15g

Filet Mignon and Mushrooms Sauce

Preparation time: 15 minutes
Cooking time: 23 minutes
Servings: 4
Ingredients:

- 1 shallot, chopped
- 2 garlic cloves, minced
- Salt and black pepper to the taste
- 2 tablespoons olive oil
- 60g of Dijon mustard
- 60ml of wine
- 4 fillet mignons
- 350ml of coconut cream
- 2 tablespoons parsley, chopped
- 12 mushrooms, sliced

Directions:

1. Heat a pan with the oil over medium-high heat. Add garlic and shallots, stir and cook for 3 minutes.
2. Add mushrooms, stir and heat for 4 minutes more.
3. Add wine, stir and cook until it evaporates.
4. Add coconut cream, mustard, parsley, a pinch of salt, and black pepper to the taste, stir, cook for 6 minutes more and take off the heat.
5. Season the fillets with salt, pepper, and place them in an air fryer. Heat at 180°C for 10 minutes.
6. Place fillets on plates, and then add the prepared mushroom sauce.

Nutrition: Calories 330, fat 10g, fibre 3g, carbs 15g, protein 20g

Beef Brisket and Onion Sauce

Preparation time: 15 minutes
Cooking time: 2 hours
Servings: 4
Ingredients:

- 2kg beef brisket
- 1kg of yellow onion, chopped
- 500g celery, chopped
- 1kg of carrot, chopped
- 8 earl grey tea bags
- Salt and black pepper to the taste
- 1L of water

For the sauce:

- 500g of canned tomatoes, chopped
- 500g of sweet onion, chopped
- 230g celery, chopped
- 30g of garlic, minced
- 230ml of white vinegar
- 115ml of vegetable oil
- 210g of brown sugar
- 8 earl grey tea bags

Directions:

1. Heat the water in an oven-safe dish. Add celery, onion, carrots, celery and salt. Stir and reduce heat to medium.
2. Combine beef brisket with 8 tea bags. Stir, then transfer to an air fryer. Heat at 150°C for 1 hour 30 minutes.
3. While the vegetable oil is heating, heat a large pan. Add the onion and stir.
4. Add the garlic, celery and tomatoes, as well as sugar, vinegar, salt and pepper to 8 tea bags. Stir, then bring to a boil. Cook for 10 minutes, then remove tea bags.

5. Place beef brisket on a cutting board. Slice, then divide between plates. Drizzle onion sauce over the top.

Nutrition: Calories 350, fat 10g, fibre 5g, carbs 40g, protein 35g

Beef Strips with Snow Peas and Mushrooms

Preparation time: 15 minutes
Cooking time: 22 minutes
Servings: 4
Ingredients:
- 2 beef steaks, cut into strips
- 1 yellow onion, cut into rings
- Salt and black pepper to the taste
- 200g of snow peas
- 230g white mushrooms, halved
- 1 teaspoon olive oil
- 2 tablespoons soy sauce

Directions:
1. Combine olive oil and soy sauce in a bowl. Whisk, then add the beef strips.
2. Combine snow peas with onion and mushrooms in a bowl. Toss in oil and salt. Heat in an air fryer for 16 minutes at 175°C.
3. Add the beef strips to the saucepan and continue cooking at 200°C for 6 more minutes.
4. Place everything on plates and then serve.

Nutrition: Calories 230, fat 10g, fibre 4g, carbs 20g protein 25g

Garlic Lamb Chops

Preparation time: 10 minutes
Cooking time: 10 minutes
Servings: 4
Ingredients:
- 2 tablespoons olive oil
- 1 tablespoon coriander, chopped
- 8 lamb chops
- 4 garlic cloves, minced
- Salt and black pepper to the taste
- 1 tablespoon oregano, chopped

Directions:
1. Combine oregano, salt, pepper and oil with the lamb chops. Toss them in a bowl.
2. Place lamb chops in your air fryer. Heat at 200°C for 10 minutes.
3. Place lamb chops on plates.
4. Serve with side salad.

Nutrition: Calories 230, fat 9g, fibre 5g, carbs 15g, protein 20g

Pork Chops and Sage Sauce

Preparation time: 10 minutes
Cooking time: 18 minutes
Servings: 2
Ingredients:

- 2 pork chops
- Salt and black pepper to the taste
- 1 tablespoon of olive oil
- 2 tablespoons of butter
- 1 shallot, sliced
- 1 handful of sage, chopped
- 1 teaspoon of lemon juice

Directions:

1. Season the pork chops evenly with salt, pepper and oil. Heat your air fryer to 190°C for 10 minutes. Flip them halfway through.
2. While the butter is heating, add the shallot to a saucepan and stir.
3. Stir in the lemon juice and sage.
4. Place the pork chops on plates. Drizzle the sage sauce over them and then serve. Enjoy!

Nutrition: Calories 269, fat 8g, fibre 10g, carbs 17g, protein 10g

Beef Kabobs

Preparation time: 10 minutes
Cooking time: 10 minutes
Servings: 4
Ingredients:

- 2 red bell peppers, chopped
- 1kg of sirloin steak, cut into medium pieces
- 1 red onion, chopped
- 1 courgette, sliced
- Juice from 1 lime
- 2 tablespoons of chili powder
- 2 tablespoons of hot sauce
- ½ tablespoons of cumin, ground
- 60ml of olive oil
- 60ml of salsa
- Salt and black pepper to the taste

Directions:

1. Mix lime juice with salsa and, oil, hot sauce, cumin, salt, chili powder, and black pepper in a bowl and whisk well.
2. Divide meat bell peppers, sliced courgette, and the red onion on skewers, rub kabobs with the salsa mix you made earlier, place in the preheated air-fryer, and air fry them for 10 minutes at 190°C flipping kabobs halfway.
3. Divide on plates and serve with a side salad.

Nutrition: Calories 175, fat 6g, fibre 4g, carbs 15g, protein 17g

FISH & SEAFOOD RECIPES

Salmon and Avocado Salsa

Preparation time: 25 minutes
Cooking time: 10 minutes
Servings: 4
Ingredients:

- 8 salmon fillets
- 1 tablespoon olive oil
- Salt and black pepper to the taste
- 1 teaspoon cumin, ground
- 1 teaspoon sweet paprika
- ½ teaspoon chili powder
- 1 teaspoon garlic powder

For the salsa:

- 1 small red onion, chopped
- 1 avocado, pitted, peeled, and chopped
- 2 tablespoons cilantro, chopped
- Juice from 2 limes
- Salt and black pepper to the taste

Directions:

1. Mix salt, pepper, chili powder, onion powder, paprika, and cumin in a bowl, stir, rub salmon with this mix, drizzle the oil, rub again, transfer to the tower air fryer and cook at 175°C for 5 minutes on each side.
2. Meanwhile, in a bowl, mix avocado with red onion, salt, pepper, cilantro, and lime juice and stir.
3. Divide fillets on plates, top with avocado salsa, and serve.

Nutrition: Calories 285, fat 15g, fibre 5g, carbs 20g, protein 18g

Shrimp and Cauliflower

Preparation time: 12 min
Cooking time: 10 min
Servings: 4
Ingredients:

- 1 tablespoon butter
- Cooking spray
- 1 cauliflower head, riced
- 500g of shrimp, peeled and deveined
- 60ml of heavy cream
- 230g of mushrooms, roughly chopped
- A pinch of red pepper flakes
- Salt and black pepper to the taste
- 2 garlic cloves, minced
- 4 bacon slices, cooked and crumbled
- 100ml of beef stock
- 1 tablespoon of parsley, finely chopped
- 1 tablespoon of chives, chopped

Directions:

1. Season shrimp with salt and pepper, spray with cooking oil, place in your air fryer, and cook at 175°C for 7 minutes.
2. Meanwhile, heat a pan with the butter over low heat, add mushrooms, stir and cook for 3-4 minutes.
3. Add garlic, cauliflower rice, pepper flakes, stock, cream, chives, parsley, salt, and pepper, stir, cook for a few minutes and take off the heat.
4. Divide shrimp on plates, add cauliflower mix on the side, sprinkle bacon on top, and serve.

Nutrition: Calories 245, fat 8g, fibre 5g, carbs 7g, protein 22g

Cod with Pearl Onions

Preparation time: 12 min
Cooking time: 15 min
Servings: 2

Ingredients:
- 400g of pearl onions
- 2 medium cod fillets
- 1 tablespoon parsley, dried
- 1 teaspoon thyme, dried
- Black pepper to the taste
- 230g of mushrooms, sliced

Directions:
1. Put fish in a heatproof pan that fits the tower air fryer, add onions, mushrooms, parsley, thyme, and black pepper, stir well, put in your air fryer, cook at 180° C, and cook for 15 minutes.
2. Divide everything on plates and serve. Enjoy!

Nutrition: Calories 272, fat 14g, fibre 9g, carbs 15g, protein 20g

Air Fried Branzino

Preparation time: 15 min
Cooking time: 10 min
Servings: 4
Ingredients:
- Zest from 1 lemon, grated
- Zest from 1 orange, grated
- Juice from ½ lemon
- Juice from ½ orange
- Salt and black pepper to the taste
- 4 medium branzino fillets, boneless
- 30g of parsley, chopped
- 2 tablespoons olive oil
- A pinch of red pepper flakes, crushed

Directions:
1. Mix fish fillets in a large bowl with lemon zest, orange zest and lemon juice. Add salt and pepper to taste. Then transfer to your preheated oven at 175°C and bake for 10 mins, flipping once.
2. Place fish on separate plates. Sprinkle with parsley and serve immediately. Enjoy!

Nutrition: Calories 265, fat 10, fibre 15g, carbs 20g, protein 10g

Coconut Tilapia

Preparation time: 12 min
Cooking time: 10 min
Servings: 4

Ingredients:

- 4 medium tilapia fillets
- 2 garlic cloves, chopped
- Salt and black pepper to the taste
- 120ml of coconut milk
- ½ jalapeno, chopped
- Cooking spray
- 1 teaspoon ginger, grated
- 15g of coriander, chopped
- ½ teaspoon garam masala

Directions:

1. Mix coconut milk with ginger, jalapeno, garlic, coriander, garam masala, and salt in a food processor.
2. Spray the fish with cooking spray and spread coconut mixture all over. Rub well. Transfer to an air fryer basket and heat at 200°C for 10 minutes.
3. Divide on several plates and serve. Enjoy!

Nutrition: Calories 200, fat 5g, fibre 7g, carbs 22g, protein 25g

Tilapia and Chives Sauce

Preparation time: 12 min
Cooking time: 8 minutes
Servings: 4
Ingredients:

- 4 medium tilapia fillets
- Cooking spray
- Juice from 1 lemon
- 2 teaspoons honey
- Salt and black pepper to the taste
- 70g of Greek yogurt
- 2 tablespoons chives, chopped

Directions:

1. Season the fish with salt and pepper, spray with cooking spray.
2. Place the seasoned fish in the preheated air fryer at 175° C, and cook for 8 minutes, flipping halfway.
3. Meanwhile, mix yogurt with honey, salt, pepper, chives, and extracted lemon juice in a bowl and whisk well.
4. Divide air fried fish on plates, drizzle yogurt sauce, and serve immediately.

Nutrition: Calories 260, fat 10g, fibre 15g, carbs 22g, protein 20g

Stuffed Calamari

Preparation time: 12 min
Cooking time: 25 minutes
Servings: 4
Ingredients:

- 110g of kale, chopped
- 4 big calamari with tentacles separated and chopped, and tubes reserved
- 1 tablespoon olive oil
- 2 tablespoons parsley, chopped
- 2 garlic cloves, minced
- 1 red bell pepper, chopped
- 50ml of canned tomato puree
- 1 yellow onion, chopped
- Salt and black pepper to the taste

Directions:

1. Heat 2 tablespoon olive oil in a large pot over low heat. Add onion and garlic and stir.

2. Stir in bell pepper, tomato puree and calamari tentacles. Add salt and pepper. Stir, and cook for three minutes.
3. Fill calamari tubes using this mixture, secure them with toothpicks and place them in an air fryer at 180°C for 20 minutes.
4. Place calamari on two plates and sprinkle with parsley.

Nutrition: Calories 320, fat 12g, fibre 15g, carbs 15g, protein 20g

Salmon and Blackberry Glaze

Preparation time: 10 min
Cooking time: 35 minutes
Servings: 4
Ingredients:
- 4 medium salmon fillets, skinless
- 250ml of water
- 1-inch ginger piece, grated
- Juice from ½ lemon
- 340g of blackberries
- 1 tablespoon olive oil
- 50g of sugar
- Salt and black pepper to the taste

Directions:
1. Heat the water in a saucepan over medium heat. Add ginger, lemon juice and blackberries. Stir, then reduce heat to low. Once boiled, simmer for about 4-5 mins.
2. Remove the mix from heat and strain into a bowl.
3. Combine the ingredients and bring to a boil over medium heat. Cook for 20 minutes.
4. Let the blackberry sauce cool, then brush the salmon with it. Season with salt and pepper and drizzle olive oil all over. Rub the fish with the oil.
5. Preheat the air fryer to 180°C. Once it is preheated, place the fish in the fryer and let it cook for 10 minutes. Flip once.
6. Divide the blackberry sauce among several plates and drizzle some on top.

Nutrition: Calories 312, fat 5g, fibre 10g, carbs 20g, protein 15g

Creamy Shrimp and Veggies

Preparation time: 10 min
Cooking time: 30 minutes
Servings: 4
Ingredients:
- 230g of mushrooms, chopped
- 1 asparagus bunch, cut into medium pieces
- 500g of shrimp, peeled and deveined
- Salt and black pepper to the taste
- 1 spaghetti squash, cut into halves
- 2 tablespoons olive oil
- 2 teaspoons Italian seasoning
- 1 yellow onion, chopped
- 1 teaspoon red pepper flakes, crushed
- 60g of butter, melted
- 50g of parmesan cheese, grated
- 2 garlic cloves, minced
- 230ml of heavy cream

Directions:
1. Place squash halves in your air fryer's basket, cook at 190°C for 17 minutes, transfer to a cutting board, scoop insides and transfer to a bowl.
2. Put water in a pot, add some salt, bring to a boil over low heat, add asparagus, steam for a couple of minutes, transfer to a bowl filled with ice water, drain and leave aside as well.
3. Heat a pan that fits your air fryer with the oil over medium heat, add onions and mushrooms, stir and cook for 7 minutes.

4. Add pepper flakes, Italian seasoning, salt, squash, asparagus, shrimp, melted butter, cream, parmesan, and garlic, toss and cook in your air fryer at 180°C for 6 minutes.
5. Divide everything on plates and serve.

Nutrition: Calories 320, fat 5g, fibre 6g, carbs 15g, protein 15g

Tasty Pollock

Preparation time: 10 min
Cooking time: 15 minutes
Servings: 4
Ingredients:
- Cooking spray
- 120ml of sour cream
- 4 Pollock fillets, boneless
- Salt and black pepper
- 25g of parmesan, grated
- 2 tablespoons butter, melted

Directions:
1. Combine sour cream, butter, parmesan and salt in a bowl. Whisk well.
2. Spray the fish with cooking spray, and season it with salt and pepper.
3. Spread the sour cream mixture on one side of each Pollock filet and place them in your preheated oven at 160°C. Cook them for 15 minutes.
4. Divide Pollock fillets and place them on plates. Serve with a side salad. Enjoy!

Nutrition: Calories 310, fat 15g, fibre 5g, carbs 15g, protein 45g

Special Catfish Filets

Preparation time: 10 min
Cooking time: 15 minutes
Servings: 2
Ingredients:
- 2 catfish filets
- ½ teaspoon garlic, minced
- 60g of butter
- 120g of Worcestershire sauce
- ½ teaspoon jerk seasoning
- 1 teaspoon mustard
- 1 tablespoon balsamic vinegar
- 120ml of catsup
- Salt and black pepper to the taste
- 1 tablespoon parsley, chopped

Directions:
1. Heat a pan with the butter over medium heat. Add Worcestershire sauce, garlic, jerk seasoning, mustard, catsup, vinegar, salt, and pepper, stir well, take off the heat and add fish fillets.
2. Toss well, leave aside for 10 minutes, drain filets, transfer them to your preheated air fryer's basket at 180° and cook for 8 minutes, flipping filets halfway.
3. Divide on tray, sprinkle chopped parsley on top, and serve right away. Enjoy!

Nutrition: Calories 350, fat 6, fibre 15g, carbs 28g, protein 18g

Marinated Salmon

Preparation time: 1 hour
Cooking time: 25 minutes
Servings: 6
Ingredients:

- 1 whole salmon
- 1 tablespoon dill, chopped
- 1 tablespoon tarragon, chopped
- 1 tablespoon garlic, minced
- Juice from 2 lemons
- 1 lemon, sliced
- A pinch of salt and black pepper

Directions:

1. Combine the fish with salt, pepper, and lemon juice in a large bowl. Toss in well and place in the refrigerator for at least 1 hour.
2. Stuff salmon with garlic and lemon slices, place in your air fryer's basket, and cook at 160°C for 25 minutes.
3. Divide on tray and serve with a tasty coleslaw. Enjoy!

Nutrition: Calories 310, fat 10g, fibre 10g, carbs 18g, protein 28g

SIDES RECIPES

Aubergine Fries

Preparation time: 10 min
Cooking time: 10 minutes
Servings: 4

Ingredients:
- 1 aubergine, cut into fry shapes
- 220g of all-purpose flour
- 1 teaspoon garlic powder
- Salt and black pepper to the taste
- 2 tablespoons olive oil, divided

Directions:
1. Preheat your air fryer to 190 degrees C.
2. Mix flour with garlic powder, salt, and pepper in a bowl.
3. Dip aubergine sticks into the flour mixture until coated well. Lightly brush them with olive oil.
4. Arrange in a single layer on the air fryer.
5. Cook for 10 minutes, flipping sticks halfway.
6. Serve immediately

Nutrition: Calories 310, fat 5g, fibre 2g, carbs 6g, protein 2g

Cauliflower Cakes

Preparation time: 10 minutes
Cooking time: 10 minutes
Servings: 5
Ingredients:
- 400g of cauliflower rice
- 2 eggs
- Cooking spray
- 30g of white flour
- 50g of parmesan, grated
- Salt and black pepper to the taste

Directions:
1. Mix cauliflower rice with salt and pepper in a bowl, and stir and squeeze excess water.
2. Place cauliflower in a bowl. Add eggs, parmesan, salt, and pepper to the bowl. Form your cakes.
3. Spray your air fryer with cooking spray and heat at 200°C. Add cauliflower cakes, then cook for 10 minutes. Flip halfway through.
4. Divide the cakes onto plates. Enjoy!

Nutrition: Calories 120, fat 3g, fibre 7g, carbs 10g, protein 4g

Air Fried Asparagus

Preparation time: 10 minutes
Cooking time: 20 minutes
Servings: 5
Ingredients:
- 500g of fresh asparagus, trimmed
- 120g of feta cheese, crumbled
- 10ml of olive oil
- Salt and black pepper to the taste

- Juice from 1 lemon
- 1 teaspoon lemon zest
- 4 garlic cloves, minced
- ½ teaspoon oregano, dried
- 2 tablespoons parsley, finely chopped
- ¼ teaspoon red pepper flakes

Directions:

1. In a bowl, mix oil with lemon zest, garlic, pepper flakes and oregano and whisk.
2. Add asparagus, cheese, salt and pepper, toss, transfer to your air fryer's basket and cook at 180°C for 10 minutes.
3. Divide asparagus on plates, drizzle lemon juice and sprinkle parsley on top and serve.

Nutrition: Calories 160, fat 14g, fibre 5g, carbs 10g, protein 8g

Courgette Fries

Preparation time: 10 min
Cooking time: 12 minutes
Servings: 4
Ingredients:

- 1 courgette, cut into medium sticks
- 2 eggs, whisked
- 1 teaspoon of olive oil
- 70g of flour
- Salt and black pepper to the taste
- 120g of breadcrumbs

Directions:

1. Combine flour with salt and pepper in a bowl.
2. Mix breadcrumbs in a bowl.

3. Combine eggs with a pinch salt and pepper in a third bowl.
4. Dip courgette fries in flour, eggs, and breadcrumbs.
5. Oil your air fryer with olive oil. Heat to 200°C. Add courgetti fries. Cook for 12 minutes.
6. serve them. Enjoy!

Nutrition: calories 172, fat 4g, fibre 5g, carbs 10g, protein 4g

Potato Wedges

Preparation time: 10 minutes
Cooking time: 25 minutes
Servings: 4
Ingredients:

- 2 potatoes, cut into wedges
- 2 tablespoons sweet chili sauce
- Salt and black pepper
- 1 tablespoon olive oil

Directions:

1. Mix potato wedges with oil, salt, and pepper in a bowl, stir well, add to air fryer's basket and cook at 180°C for 25 minutes, flipping them once.
2. Divide on plates, drizzle sour cream and chili sauce all over and
3. Serve them as a side dish.

Nutrition: Calories 170, fat 9g, fibre 10g, carbs 15g, protein 9g

Onion Rings Side Dish

Preparation time: 10 minutes
Cooking time: 10 minutes
Servings: 4

Ingredients:
- 1 onion cut into medium slices and in rings
- 1 egg
- 1 teaspoon baking powder
- 150g of white flour
- 230ml of milk
- A pinch of salt
- 90g of breadcrumbs

Directions:
1. Mix flour with salt and baking powder in a bowl, stir together, dredge onion rings in this mix and place them on a separate plate.
2. Add milk and egg to the flour mix and whisk well.
3. Dip onion rings in this mixture, dip them in breadcrumbs, put them in your tower air fryer's basket, and air fry them at 180°C for 10 minutes.
4. Divide on plates and serve as a side dish for a steak.

Nutrition: Calories 145, fat 9g, fibre 22g, carbs 15g, protein 4g

Tortilla Chips

Preparation time: 12 minutes
Cooking time: 8 minutes
Servings: 6
Ingredients:
- 6 corn tortillas, cut into triangles
- A pinch of sweet paprika
- Salt and black pepper
- 1 tablespoon olive oil
- A pinch of garlic powder

Directions:
1. Combine tortilla chips with oil, add salt, pepper, garlic powder, and paprika in a bowl, stir well, place them in your air fryer's basket, and air fry them at 200°C for 8 minutes.
2. Serve them as a side for a fish dish.

Nutrition: Calories 54, fat 2g, fibre 2g, carbs 5g, protein 5g

Simple Potato Chips

Preparation time: 25 minutes
Cooking time: 25 minutes
Servings: 6
Ingredients:
- 3 potatoes, peeled into thin chips, soaked in water for 25 minutes, drained and pat dried
- 2 teaspoons rosemary, chopped
- Salt the taste
- 1 tablespoon olive oil

Directions:

1. Mix potato chips with salt and oil in a bowl, toss to coat, place the chips in your air fryer's basket and cook at 170°C for 25 minutes.
2. Divide on plates, sprinkle rosemary all over
3. serve as a side dish.

Nutrition: calories 205, fat 5g, fibre 4g, carbs 15g, protein 6g

Mushrooms and Sour Cream

Preparation time: 12 minutes
Cooking time: 12 minutes
Servings: 4
Ingredients:
- 1 bacon strips, chopped
- 250ml of sour cream
- 1 yellow onion, chopped
- 2 tablespoons of olive oil
- 1 carrot, grated
- Salt and black pepper
- 1 green bell pepper, chopped
- 24 mushrooms, stems removed
- 120g of cheddar cheese, grated

Directions:
1. Heat the 2 tablespoons of olive oil in a large pan over medium heat.
2. Add bacon, onion bell pepper, carrot and stir.
3. Stir in salt, pepper, and sour cream. Allow to cook for 1 more minute, then turn off heat. Let cool.
4. Fill mushrooms with this mixture, then sprinkle cheese over the top. Cook for 8 minutes at 180°C.

5. Divide the mixture among several plates and serve as a side-dish.

Nutrition: calories 210, fat 5g, fibre 8g, carbs 10g, protein 5g

Delicious Roasted Carrots

Preparation time: 15 minutes
Cooking time: 25 minutes
Servings: 4
Ingredients:
- 4 tablespoons orange juice
- 500g baby carrots
- 1 teaspoon herbs de Provence
- 2 teaspoons olive oil

Directions:
1. Mix carrots with herbs de Provence, oil, and orange juice in your air fryer's basket, toss and cook at 160°C for 25 minutes.
2. Divide on plates and serve as a side dish. Enjoy!

Nutrition: calories 110g, fat 3g, fibre 4g, carbs 5g, protein 5g

Cheesy Brussels Sprouts

Preparation time: 10 minutes
Cooking time: 10 minutes
Servings: 4
Ingredients:
- 500g Brussels sprouts, washed
- Juice of 1 lemon
- Salt and black pepper to the taste
- 2 tablespoons butter

- 3 tablespoons parmesan, grated

Directions:
1. Put Brussels sprouts in your air fryer, cook them at 180°C for 10 minutes and transfer them to a bowl.
2. Heat up a pan with the 2 tablespoons butter over medium heat, add lemon juice, salt and pepper, whisk well and add to Brussels sprouts.
3. Add parmesan, toss until parmesan melts.
4. Serve and enjoy

Nutrition: calories 150, fat 5g, fibre 6g, carbs 6g, protein 12g

Potatoes Patties

Preparation time: 12 minutes
Cooking time: 8 minutes
Servings: 6
Ingredients:
- 4 potatoes, boiled and mashed
- Salt and black pepper
- 120g of parmesan, grated
- A pinch of nutmeg
- 2 tablespoons white flour
- 2 egg yolks
- 3 tablespoons chives, chopped

For the breading:
- 30g of white flour
- 30g of breadcrumbs
- 2 eggs, whisked
- 3 tablespoons vegetable oil

Directions:
1. Combine mashed potatoes, egg yolks, salt and pepper with nutmeg and parmesan.

2. Add 2 tablespoons of flour. Stir well and form medium-sized cakes.
3. Combine vegetable oil and breadcrumbs in a separate bowl. Stir.
4. Whisk the eggs and flour together in a third bowl.
5. Dip the cakes in flour, then in egg and breadcrumbs, and finally, put them in an air fryer basket.
6. Cook for 8 minutes at 190°C.
7. Divide them among plates and serve them as side dishes.

Nutrition: calories 145, fat 4g, fibre 5g, carbs 18g, protein 5g

Air Fried Creamy Cabbage

Preparation time: 10 minutes
Cooking time: 22 minutes
Servings: 6
Ingredients:
- 1 green cabbage head, chopped
- 2 tablespoons cornstarch
- 1 yellow onion, chopped
- 4 bacon slices, chopped
- 220ml of whipped cream
- Salt and black pepper

Directions:
1. Place chopped cabbage, onion, and bacon in your air fryer.
2. Combine cornstarch, cream, salt, and pepper in a bowl. Stir and then add cabbage.
3. Air fry at 200°C for 22 minutes

4. Divide on plates and serve with a side dish.

Nutrition: Calories 210, fat 12g, fibre 4g, carbs 18g, protein 4g

Coconut Cream Potatoes

Preparation time: 10 minutes
Cooking time: 25 minutes
Servings: 4

Ingredients:
- 2 potatoes, sliced
- Salt and black pepper to the taste
- 2 eggs, whisked
- 1 tablespoon cheddar cheese, grated
- 1 tablespoon flour
- 118ml of coconut cream

Directions:
1. Place potato slices in your air fryer's basket and air fry at 180° C for 12 minutes.
2. Meanwhile, in a bowl, mix eggs with coconut cream, salt, pepper and flour.
3. Arrange potatoes in your air fryer's pan, add coconut cream mix over them, sprinkle cheese, return to air fryer's basket and cook at 200°C for 13 minutes more.
4. Divide on plates and serve as a side dish.

Nutrition: calories 175, fat 5g, fibre 2g, carbs 16g, protein 18g

Avocado Fries

Preparation time: 15 minutes
Cooking time: 15 minutes
Servings: 4

Ingredients:
- 60g of panko breadcrumbs
- 1 avocado, pitted, peeled, cut into medium fries
- 1 egg, whisked
- Salt and black pepper to the taste
- 1 tablespoon olive oil
- 1 tablespoon lemon juice

Directions:
1. Mix panko with salt and pepper in a bowl and stir.
2. Mix egg with a pinch of salt in another bowl and whisk.
3. Mix avocado fries with lemon juice and oil in a third bowl and toss.
4. Dip fries in egg, then in panko, place fries in the tower air fryer's basket and air fry at 200°C for 15 minutes, shaking halfway.
5. Divide on plates.

Nutrition: calories 130, fat 10g, fibre 4g, carbs 15g, protein 5g

VEGAN RECIPES

Broccoli Salad

Preparation time: 10 minutes
Cooking time: 10 minutes
Servings: 5

Ingredients:

- 1 tablespoon Chinese rice
- 1 broccoli head, florets separated
- 6 garlic cloves, minced
- 1 tablespoon peanut oil
- Salt and black pepper to the taste
- vinegar

Directions:

1. Combine the broccoli with salt, pepper and half the oil in a bowl. Toss the mixture into an air fryer. Heat at 175°C for 10 minutes. Stir the fryer halfway.
2. Place the broccoli in a bowl. Add the remaining peanut oil, garlic, rice, and vinegar to the bowl. Toss well and enjoy.

Nutrition: calories 120, fat 4g, fibre 5g, carbs 4g, protein 4g

Beets and Arugula Salad

Preparation time: 10 minutes
Cooking time: 12 minutes
Servings: 5

Ingredients:

- 20g of arugula
- 2 scallions, chopped
- 500g of beets, peeled and quartered
- 2 teaspoons mustard
- 2 teaspoons orange zest, grated
- 2 tablespoons cider vinegar
- 20ml orange juice
- 2 tablespoons brown sugar
- A drizzle of olive oil

Directions:

1. Rub beets with the olive oil and extracted orange juice, place them in the tower air fryer and cook at 175°C for 12 minutes.
2. Transfer beet quarters to a bowl, add chopped scallions, arugula and 2 teaspoons orange zest and toss.
3. In another bowl, mix mustard with vinegar, and sugar, whisk well, add to salad, toss and serve.

Nutrition: Calories 120, fat 3g, fibre 3g, carbs 10g, protein 5g

Stuffed Aubergine

Preparation time: 10 minutes
Cooking time: 35 minutes
Servings: 6

Ingredients:
- 60g of cauliflower, chopped
- 4 small aubergines, cut into halves
- 90g of feta cheese, crumbled
- 30g of parsley, chopped
- Salt and black pepper
- 10 tablespoons olive oil
- 1kg tomatoes, cut into halves and grated
- 1 green bell pepper, chopped
- 1 yellow onion, chopped
- 1 tablespoon garlic, minced
- 1 teaspoon oregano, chopped

Directions:
1. Season aubergines with salt, pepper and 4 tablespoons oil, toss, put them in your air fryer and cook at 180°C for 16 minutes.
2. Meanwhile, heat up a pan with 3 tablespoons of oil over medium high heat, add onion, stir and cook for 5 minutes.
3. Add bell pepper, garlic, and cauliflower, stir, cook for 5 minutes, take off heat, add parsley, tomato, salt, pepper, oregano and cheese and whisk everything.
4. Fill the aubergines with the vegetable mix. Drizzle the remaining oil over the vegetables, then place them in an air fryer. Cook at 180°C for 6 more minutes.
5. Divide the baked aubergines on several plates and serve immediately.

Nutrition: calories 235, fat 5g, fibre 2g, carbs 18g, protein 2g

Balsamic Potatoes

Preparation time: 10 minutes
Cooking time: 25 minutes
Servings: 4

Ingredients:
- 250g of cherry tomatoes
- 600g baby potatoes, halved
- 2 garlic cloves, chopped
- 2 red onions, chopped
- 2 thyme springs, chopped
- 3 tablespoons olive oil
- 1 ½ tablespoons balsamic vinegar
- Salt and black pepper

Directions:
1. In your food processor, mix garlic with onions, oil, vinegar, thyme, salt and pepper and pulse really well.
2. In a bowl, mix potatoes with tomatoes and balsamic marinade, toss well, transfer to your air fryer and cook at 190°C for 25 minutes.
3. Divide on plates and serve. Enjoy!

Nutrition: calories 300, fat 5g, fibre 8g, carbs 15g, protein 6g

Delicious Portobello Mushrooms

Preparation time: 10 minutes
Cooking time: 15 minutes
Servings: 4

Ingredients:
- 4 Portobello mushrooms, stems removed and chopped
- 150g of almonds, roughly chopped
- 10 basil leaves
- 30g of baby spinach
- 3 garlic cloves, chopped
- 8 cherry tomatoes, halved
- 1 tablespoon parsley
- 7ml of olive oil
- Salt and black pepper to the taste

Directions:
1. In your food processor, mix basil with spinach, garlic, almonds, parsley, oil, salt, black pepper to the taste and mushroom stems and blend well.
2. Stuff each mushroom with this mix, place them in your air fryer and cook at 180°C for 15 minutes.
3. Divide mushrooms on plates and serve.

Nutrition: Calories 140, fat 4g, fibre 2g, carbs 5g, protein 15g

Courgette Noodles Delight

Preparation time: 10 minutes
Cooking time: 25 minutes
Servings: 6

Ingredients:
- 2 courgettes, cut with a spiralizer
- 1 tablespoons olive oil
- 60g of spinach, torn
- 120g of cherry tomatoes, halved
- 500g of mushrooms, sliced
- 30g of sun-dried tomatoes, chopped
- 1 teaspoon garlic, minced
- A handful basil, chopped
- 60ml of tomatoes sauce
- Salt and black pepper

Directions:
1. Put courgette noodles in a bowl, season salt and black pepper and leave them aside for 10 minutes.
2. Heat up a pan that fits your air fryer with the oil over medium high heat, add garlic, stir and cook for 1 minute.
3. Add mushrooms, sun dried tomatoes, cherry tomatoes, spinach, cayenne, sauce and courgette noodles, stir, introduce in your air fryer and cook at 160°C for 15 minutes.
4. Divide on a tray and serve with basil sprinkled on top.

Nutrition: calories 125g, fat 1g, fibre 2g, carbs 2g, protein 10g

Stuffed Poblano Peppers

Preparation time: 10 min

Cooking time: 20 min

Servings: 4

Ingredients:

- 10 poblano peppers, tops cut off and deseeded
- 230g of mushrooms, chopped
- 2 teaspoons garlic, minced
- 1 white onion, chopped
- 10g of coriander, chopped
- 1 tablespoon of olive oil
- Salt and black pepper

Directions:

1. Heat a pan with the oil over medium-high heat, add onion and mushrooms, stir and cook for 5 minutes.
2. Add garlic, cilantro, salt and black pepper, stir and cook for 2 minutes.
3. Divide this mix into poblanos, introduce them in your air fryer and cook at 180°C for 20 minutes.
4. Divide among plates and serve.

Nutrition: calories 155, fat 4g, fibre 3g, carbs 7g, protein 10g

APPETIZERS RECIPES

Nutrition: Calories 200, fat 4g, fibre 11g, carbs 22g, protein 10g

Potato Spread

Preparation time: 15 minutes
Cooking time: 15 minutes
Servings: 6

Ingredients:
- 500g of canned garbanzo beans
- 5 garlic cloves, minced
- 400g of sweet potatoes, peeled and chopped
- 30g of tahini
- Salt and white pepper
- 2 tablespoons lemon juice
- 1 tablespoon olive oil
- ½ teaspoon cumin, ground
- 2 tablespoons water

Directions:
1. Place potatoes in the basket of the tower air fryer and cook at 180°C for 15 minutes. Let it cool down, then peel.
2. Mix sesame paste with garlic, beans, lemon juice, cumin, water, and oil, stir well
3. Add salt, pepper, stir again, then divide into bowls.
4. Serve!

Air Fried Dill Pickles

Preparation time: 12 minutes
Cooking time: 8 minutes
Servings: 6

Ingredients:
- ½ teaspoon sweet paprika
- 10ml of milk
- 500g of ounces jarred dill pickles, cut into wedges
- ½ teaspoon garlic powder
- 60g of white flour
- 1 egg
- 10ml of ranch sauce
- Cooking spray

Directions:
1. Combine milk with egg in a bowl and whisk well.
2. Mix flour with salt, ½ teaspoon garlic powder, and paprika in a second bowl and stir as well.
3. Put pickles in flour, then dip in the egg mix, and again dip in flour and place them in the tower air fryer.
4. Apply cooking spray on them, cook pickle wedges at 200°C for 8 minutes, transfer to a bowl and serve with ranch sauce on the side.

Nutrition: Calories 110, fat 3g, fibre 4g, carbs 12g, protein 5g

Crisp Shrimp

Preparation time: 12 minutes
Cooking time: 10 minutes
Servings: 6

Ingredients:
- 100g of coconut, shredded
- 12 big shrimp, deveined and peeled
- 2 egg whites
- 120g of white flour
- Salt and black pepper
- 150g of panko breadcrumbs
- Salt and black pepper

Directions:
1. In a bowl, mix 150g of panko breadcrumbs with coconut and stir.
2. Put flour, salt, and pepper in another bowl and whisk 2 egg whites in a third one.
3. Put shrimp in flour, egg whites mix and coconut, place them all in the tower air fryer's basket, cook at 180°C for 10 minutes flipping halfway.
4. Place on a tray and serve as an appetizer.

Nutrition: Calories 140, fat 4g, fibre 0g, carbs 3g, protein 4g

Sweet Popcorn

Preparation time: 8 minutes
Cooking time: 12 minutes
Servings: 5
Ingredients:
- 5 tablespoons corn kernels
- 60g of brown sugar
- 2 ½ tablespoons butter

Directions:
1. Place corn kernels in an air fryer pan. Heat at 200°C for 6 minutes. Transfer to a tray and let cool.
2. Heat the 2 ½ tablespoons butter in a large pan over low heat. Stir until it melts.
3. Toss the popcorn on the tray, then heat up.
4. Let cool down. Divide into bowls and enjoy as a snack.

Nutrition: Calories 75, fat 1g, fibre 1g, carbs 1g, protein 1g

Salmon Meatballs

Preparation time: 10 minutes
Cooking time: 12 minutes
Servings: 5
Ingredients:
- Cooking spray
- Salt and black pepper
- 3 tablespoons cilantro, minced
- ½ teaspoon paprika
- 1 small yellow onion, chopped
- 500g salmon, skinless and chopped
- 1 egg white
- 2 garlic cloves, minced
- 30g of panko
- ½ teaspoon oregano, ground

Directions:

1. Combine salmon with onion, garlic, egg white, ginger, oregano, salt, pepper, and cloves.
2. Mix in panko and form meatballs with your hands.
3. Put them in the tower air fryer basket. Spray with cooking spray. Cook at 160°C for 12 minutes, shaking the fryer halfway.
4. Place meatballs on a platter and serve as an appetizer.

Nutrition: calories 290, fat 10g, fibre 4g, carbs 20g, protein 20g

Chicken Breast Rolls

Preparation time: 12 minutes
Cooking time: 20 minutes
Servings: 4

Ingredients:
- 60g of baby spinach
- 4 chicken breasts, boneless and skinless
- 60g of sun-dried tomatoes, chopped
- Salt and black pepper
- 1½ tablespoons Italian seasoning
- 4 mozzarella slices
- A drizzle of olive oil

Directions:
1. Flatten the 4 chicken breasts using a meat tenderizer, mix the sun-dried tomatoes, 4 mozzarella slices and spinach, season with salt, pepper, and Italian seasoning, roll and seal them.
2. Place them in your air fryer's basket, drizzle some oil over them and cook at 190°C for 20 minutes, flipping once.
3. Arrange chicken rolls on a platter and serve them as an appetizer.

Nutrition: calories 310, fat 2g, fibre 5g, carbs 8g, protein 1g

Crispy Radish Chips

Preparation time: 12 minutes
Cooking time: 12 minutes
Servings: 5
Ingredients:
- 1 tablespoon chives, chopped
- Cooking spray
- Salt and black pepper
- 15 radishes, sliced

Directions:
1. Arrange radish slices in your air fryer's basket, spray them with cooking oil, season with black pepper and salt to the taste,
2. Cook them at 180°C for 12 minutes, flipping them halfway.
3. Transfer to bowls and serve with chives sprinkled on top.

Nutrition: calories 80, fat 2g, fibre 2g, carbs 3g, protein 2g

Crab Sticks

Preparation time: 12 minutes
Cooking time: 12 minutes
Servings: 5

Ingredients:
- 10 crabsticks, halved
- 2 teaspoons Cajun seasoning
- 2 teaspoons sesame oil

Directions:

1. Put crab sticks in a bowl, add sesame oil and Cajun seasoning, toss, transfer them to your air fryer's basket and cook at 180°C for 12 minutes.
2. Arrange on a platter and serve as an appetizer.

Nutrition: calories 110, fat 0g, fibre 2g, carbs 5g, protein 3g

Fish Nuggets

Preparation time: 10 minutes
Cooking time: 10 minutes
Servings: 4
Ingredients:

- 350g of fish fillets, cut into medium pieces
- Lemon juice from ½ lemon
- Salt and black pepper to the taste
- Cooking spray
- 5 tablespoons flour
- 1 egg, whisked
- 4 tablespoons homemade mayonnaise
- 5 tablespoons water
- 90g of panko breadcrumbs
- 1 tablespoon garlic powder
- 1 tablespoon smoked paprika
- 1 teaspoon dill, dried

Directions:

1. Combine flour and water in a bowl. Stir well.
2. Combine egg, salt, and water and mix well.

3. Combine panko, garlic powder and paprika in a separate bowl. Stir well.
4. Dip the fish in flour, egg, and panko mixture, then place them in an air fryer basket. Spray with cooking oil, and let them cook for 10 minutes at 200°C.
5. In a large bowl, combine mayo with lemon juice and dill. Mix well.
6. Place fish nuggets on tray and serve with dill Mayo.

Nutrition: calories 320, fat 10g, fibre 8g, carbs 18g, protein 14g

Jalapeno Balls

Preparation time: 15 minutes
Cooking time: 4 minutes
Servings:
Ingredients:

- 90g of cream cheese
- 3 bacon slices, cooked and crumbled
- ¼ teaspoon onion powder
- 1 jalapeno pepper, chopped
- Salt and black pepper to the taste
- ½ teaspoon parsley, dried
- ¼ teaspoon garlic powder

Directions:

1. In a bowl, mix cream cheese with jalapeno pepper, onion and garlic powder, parsley, bacon salt and pepper and stir well.
2. Shape small balls out of this mix, place them in your air fryer's basket, cook at 180°C for 4 minutes, arrange on a platter and serve as an appetizer.

Nutrition: calories 175, fat 5g, fibre 2g, carbs 10g, protein 6g

SNACKS RECIPES

Coconut Chicken Bites

Preparation time: 12 minutes
Cooking time: 10 minutes
Servings: 4
Ingredients:

- 1 teaspoons garlic powder
- 8 chicken tenders
- 2 eggs
- 150g of coconut, shredded
- Salt and black pepper
- 75g of panko breadcrumbs
- Cooking spray

Directions:

1. Combine eggs with salt, pepper, and garlic powder in a bowl. Mix well.
2. Combine coconut and panko in a separate bowl. Stir well.
3. Dip chicken tenders into egg mix, then coat with coconut one-by-one.
4. Spray chicken bits with the cooking spray and place in an air fryer basket. Heat for 10 minutes at 175°C.
5. Place them on a tray and serve as an appetizer.

Nutrition: calories 252, fat 5g, fibre 3g, carbs 15g, protein 25g

Courgette Chips

Preparation time: 12 minutes
Cooking time: 1 hour
Servings: 5
Ingredients:

- 2 courgettes, thinly sliced
- Salt and black pepper to the taste
- 2 tablespoons olive oil
- 2 tablespoons balsamic vinegar

Directions:

1. In a bowl, mix oil with vinegar, salt and pepper and whisk well.
2. Add courgette slices, toss to coat well, introduce in your air fryer and cook at 130°C for 1 hour.
3. Serve Courgette chips cold as a snack.

Nutrition: calories 45, fat 4g, fibre 8g, carbs 4g, protein 8g

Chickpeas Snack

Preparation time: 10 minutes
Cooking time: 12 minutes
Servings: 4
Ingredients:

- 1kg of canned chickpeas, drained
- ½ teaspoon cumin, ground 1 tablespoon olive oil
- 1 teaspoon smoked paprika
- Salt and black pepper to the taste

Directions:

1. In a bowl, mix chickpeas with oil, cumin, paprika, salt and pepper, toss to coat, place them in your fryer's basket and cook at 200°C for 12 minutes.
2. Divide into parts and serve as a snack.

Nutrition: Calories 145, fat 2g, fibre 7g, carbs 22g, protein 8g

Banana Chips

Preparation time: 10 minutes
Cooking time: 20 minutes
Servings: 6
Ingredients:
- 1 teaspoon olive oil
- 6 bananas, peeled and sliced
- A pinch of salt
- ½ teaspoon chaat masala
- ½ teaspoon turmeric powder

Directions:
1. Mix banana slices with salt, turmeric, chaat masala and oil in a bowl, toss and leave aside for 10 minutes.
2. Transfer banana slices to the preheated air fryer at 182°C and cook them for 20 minutes flipping them once.
3. Serve as a snack. Enjoy!

Nutrition: calories 120, fat 2g, fibre 2g, carbs 4g, protein 3g

Spring Rolls

Preparation time: 10 minutes
Cooking time: 22 minutes
Servings: 4
Ingredients:
- 200g of green cabbage, shredded
- 2 tablespoons corn flour
- 2 yellow onions, chopped
- 1 carrot, grated
- 1 teaspoon soy sauce
- ½ chili pepper, minced
- 1 tablespoon ginger, grated
- 2 tablespoons water
- 3 garlic cloves, minced
- 1 teaspoon sugar
- Salt and black pepper
- 2 tablespoons olive oil
- 10 spring roll sheets

Directions:
1. Heat oil in a large saucepan. Add cabbage, onions, chili pepper, ginger, garlic, sugar, soy sauce, salt, and carrots.
2. Make spring roll sheets by cutting them into squares. Divide the cabbage mixture on each one and then roll them.
3. Combine corn flour and water in a bowl. Stir well, then seal the spring rolls using this mixture.
4. Put spring rolls in an air fryer basket and bake them for 10 minutes at 180°C.
5. Cook the flip rolls for 12 more minutes.
6. Assemble the ingredients on a platter. Serve them as an appetizer.

Nutrition: calories 214, fat 5g, fibre 4g, carbs 10g, protein 5g

Cheesy Courgette Snack

Preparation time: 10 minutes
Cooking time: 10 minutes
Servings: 4
- **Ingredients:**
- 120g of mozzarella, shredded
- A pinch of cumin
- 30g of tomato sauce
- Salt and black pepper
- 1 courgette, sliced
- Cooking spray

Directions:
1. Arrange courgette slices in your air fryer's basket, spray them with cooking oil, spread tomato sauce all over, them, season with salt, pepper, cumin, sprinkle mozzarella at the end and cook them at 170°C for 10 minutes.
2. Arrange them on a platter and serve as a snack.

Nutrition: calories 150, fat 5g, fibre 3g, carbs 10g, protein 5g

Pesto Crackers

Preparation time: 12 minutes
Cooking time: 20 minutes
Servings: 4
Ingredients:
- 180g of flour
- 1 tablespoons basil pesto
- ½ teaspoon baking powder
- ¼ teaspoon basil, dried
- Salt and black pepper
- 1 garlic clove, minced
- 3 tablespoons butter
Directions:

1. In a bowl, mix salt, pepper, baking powder, flour, garlic, cayenne, basil, pesto, and butter and stir until you obtain a dough.
2. Spread this dough on a lined baking sheet that fits your air fryer, introduce in the fryer at 165°C and bake for 20 minutes.
3. Leave aside to cool down, cut crackers and serve them as a snack.

Nutrition: calories 210, fat 22g, fibre 1g, carbs 5g, protein 7g

Cheese Sticks

Preparation time: 1 hour and 15 minutes
Cooking time: 10 minutes
Servings: 16
Ingredients:
- 8 mozzarella cheese strings, cut into halves
- 1 egg, whisked
- 1 garlic clove, minced
- Salt and black pepper
- 1 tablespoon Italian seasoning
- 50g of parmesan, grated
- Cooking spray
Directions:
1. In a bowl, mix parmesan with salt, pepper, Italian seasoning, and garlic and stir well.
2. Put whisked eggs in another bowl.
3. Dip mozzarella sticks in egg mixture, then in cheese mix.
4. Dip them again in egg and in parmesan mix and keep them in the freezer for 1 hour.
5. Spray cheese sticks with cooking oil, place them in your air fryer's basket and cook at

200°C for 10 minutes flipping them halfway.

6. Arrange them on a platter and serve as a snack.

Nutrition: calories 145, fat 6g, fibre 1g, carbs 4g, protein 5g

Empanadas

Preparation time: 1 hour and 15 minutes
Cooking time: 30 minutes
Servings: 16
Ingredients:

- 1 package empanada shells
- 1 green bell pepper, chopped
- 1 egg yolk whisked
- 1 tablespoon olive oil
- 500g of beef meat
- ½ teaspoon cumin, ground
- 1 yellow onion, chopped
- Salt and black pepper
- 2 garlic cloves, minced
- 60g of tomato salsa
- 1 egg yolk whisked
- 1 tablespoon water

Directions:

1. Heat the 1 tablespoon olive oil in a pan over medium-high heat. Add beef and brown on all sides.
2. Add onion, garlic, salt, pepper, bell pepper and tomato salsa, stir and cook for 15 minutes.
3. Divide cooked meat in empanada shells, brush them with egg wash and seal.
4. Place them in your air fryer's steamer basket and cook at 180° C for 15 minutes.
5. Arrange on a platter and serve as a snack.

Nutrition: calories 270, fat 15g, fibre 15g, carbs 21g, protein 8g

Sausage Balls

Preparation time: 15 minutes
Cooking time: 20 minutes
Servings: 16
Ingredients:

- 3 tablespoons breadcrumbs
- 120g sausage meat,
- ½ teaspoon garlic, minced
- Salt and black pepper
- 1 teaspoon sage
- 1 small onion, chopped

Directions:

1. In a bowl, mix sausage with salt, pepper, sage, garlic, onion, and breadcrumbs, stir well and shape small balls out of this mix.
2. Put them in your air fryer's basket, cook at 185°C for 20 minutes, cut into different bowls and serve as a snack.

Nutrition: calories 135, fat 8g, fibre 1g, carbs 12g, protein 5g

DESSERTS RECIPES

Crispy Apples

Preparation time: 10 minutes
Cooking time: 12 minutes
Servings: 5

Ingredients:
- 5 apples, cored and cut into chunks
- 70g of old-fashioned rolled oats
- 1 teaspoon cinnamon powder
- 4 tablespoons butter
- ½ teaspoon nutmeg powder
- 1 tablespoon maple syrup
- 15ml water
- 35g of flour
- 60g of brown sugar

Directions:
1. Put the apples in a pan that fits your air fryer, add cinnamon, nutmeg, maple syrup and water.
2. In a bowl, mix butter with oats, sugar, salt, and flour, stir, drop spoonfuls of this mix on top of apples, introduce in your air fryer and cook at 175°C for 12 minutes.
3. Serve warm.

Nutrition: calories 205, fat 6g, fibre 7g, carbs 28g, protein 10g

Ginger Cheesecake

Preparation time: 2 hours
Cooking time: 25 minutes
Servings: 3

Ingredients:
- ½ teaspoon vanilla extract
- ½ teaspoon nutmeg,
- 2 teaspoons butter, melted
- 70g of sugar
- 500g of cream cheese, soft
- 2 eggs
- 1 teaspoon rum
- 120g of ginger cookies, crumbled

Directions:
1. Grease a large pan with butter and then sprinkle cookie crumbs to the bottom.
2. Beat cream cheese with vanilla, eggs, rum, and nutmeg in a bowl. Spread the mixture over the cookie crumbs.
3. Place mixture in an air fryer for 25 minutes at 170°C.
4. Let the cheesecake cool in the refrigerator for at least 2 hours before cutting and serving.

Nutrition: calories 410, fat 10g, fibre 8g, carbs 16g, protein 6g

Blueberry Scones

Preparation time: 15 minutes
Cooking time: 15 minutes
Servings: 5

Ingredients:
- 120g of white flour
- 120g of heavy cream
- 150g of blueberries
- 5 tablespoons sugar
- 2 eggs
- 120g of butter
- 2 teaspoons baking powder
- 2 teaspoons vanilla extract

Directions:
1. In a bowl, mix flour, salt, baking powder and blueberries and stir.
2. In another bowl, mix heavy cream with butter, vanilla extract, sugar, and eggs and stir well.
3. Combine the 2 mixtures, knead until you obtain your dough, shape 10 triangles from this mix, place them on a lined baking sheet that fits your air fryer and cook them at 160°C for 15 minutes.
4. Serve them cold.

Nutrition: calories 135, fat 2g, fibre 2g, carbs 5g, protein 4g

Strawberry Shortcakes

Preparation time: 30 minutes
Cooking time: 22 minutes
Servings: 5

Ingredients:
- 1 teaspoon lime zest, grated
- 200g of flour
- 50g of sugar + 4 tablespoons
- 1 teaspoon baking powder
- 1 egg, whisked
- 120ml of whipping cream
- ¼ teaspoon baking soda
- Cooking spray
- 80g of butter
- 230g of buttermilk
- 1 tablespoon rum
- 1 tablespoon mint, chopped
- 250g of strawberries, sliced

Directions:
1. Combine flour, 1/4 of sugar, baking powder, and baking soda in a bowl. Stir.
2. Combine buttermilk and egg in another bowl. Stir, then add the flour mixture to the bowl.
3. Pour the dough into 6 jars coated with cooking spray. Cover them with foil and place them in an air fryer.
4. Cook at 190°C for 22 minutes.
5. In a large bowl, combine strawberries with 3 tablespoons of sugar and rum. Add mint, lime zest, and rum. Stir and let cool in a refrigerator.
6. Combine whipping cream and 1 tablespoon of sugar in a separate bowl. Stir.
7. Remove jars, divide the strawberry mixture among them, then top with whipped cream and serve. Enjoy!

Nutrition: calories 165, fat 2g, fibre 4g, carbs 5g, protein 2g

Sweet Potato Cheesecake

Preparation time: 10 minutes
Cooking time: 10 minutes
Servings: 5
Ingredients:
- 4 tablespoons butter, melted
- 50ml of sweet potato puree
- 170g of mascarpone, soft
- 1 teaspoon vanilla extract
- 60g of graham crackers, crumbled
- 230g of cream cheese, soft
- 25ml of milk
- ¼ teaspoons cinnamon powder

Directions:
1. In a bowl, mix butter with crumbled crackers, stir well, press on the bottom of a cake pan that fits your air fryer and keep in the fridge for now.
2. In another bowl, mix cream cheese with mascarpone, sweet potato puree, milk, cinnamon and vanilla and whisk really well.
3. Spread this over crust, place in your air fryer, cook at 150°C for 10 minutes and keep in the fridge for a few hours before serving.

Nutrition: calories 170, fat 5g, fibre 6g, carbs 6g, protein 4g

Cocoa Cookies

Preparation time: 10 minutes
Cooking time: 10 minutes

Servings: 5
Ingredients:
- 90g of cocoa powder
- 110g of cream cheese
- 180ml of coconut oil, melted
- ½ teaspoon baking powder
- 6 eggs
- 2 teaspoons vanilla
- 5 tablespoons sugar

Directions:
1. Combine eggs, coconut oil, baking powder, cocoa powder, and vanilla in a blender. Mix the cream cheese, vanilla, and cream cheese with a mixer.
2. Transfer the mixture to a lined baking tray that will fit your air fryer. Heat at 160°C and bake for 15 min.
3. Cut cookie sheets into rectangular shapes and serve.

Nutrition: calories 175, fat 15, fibre 2g, carbs 3g, protein 4g

Bread Pudding

Preparation time: 12 minutes
Cooking time: 50 minutes
Servings: 3
Ingredients:
- 80g of chocolate chips
- 50g of sugar
- 140g of cherries
- 8 glazed doughnuts, crumbled
- 120g of whipping cream
- 4 egg yolks
- 80g of raisins

Directions:
1. Combine the cherries with the egg yolks and whipping cream in a bowl. Stir well.
2. Mix raisins, sugar, chocolate chips, and doughnuts in a bowl. Stir.
3. Mix the two mixtures, then transfer to a greased skillet that will fit your air fryer. Heat at 160°C for 50 minutes.

4. Before cutting into the pudding, chill it. Enjoy!

Nutrition: calories 300, fat 6g, fibre 2g, carbs 25g, protein 10g

Tasty Banana Cake

Preparation time: 5 minutes
Cooking time: 20 minutes
Servings: 4
Ingredients:

- ½ teaspoon cinnamon powder
- 120g of white flour
- 1 tablespoon butter, soft
- 1 banana, peeled and mashed
- 2 tablespoons honey
- 1 egg
- 65g of brown sugar
- Cooking spray
- 1 teaspoon baking powder

Directions:

1. Spray a pan with cooking spray and set aside.
2. Combine butter, sugar, honey, banana, egg, baking powder, and cinnamon in a bowl. Then, whisk.
3. Combine the ingredients in a greased cake pan and spray with cooking oil.
4. Heat in your air fryer for 20 minutes at 180°C.
5. Allow the cake to cool, then slice and enjoy.

Nutrition: calories 230, fat 5g, fibre 1g, carbs 30g, protein 4g

Air Fried Apples

Preparation time: 10 minutes
Cooking time: 18 minutes
Servings: 4
Ingredients:

- 2 big apples, cored
- 1 tablespoon cinnamon
- A handful raisins
- Raw honey to the taste

Directions:

1. Fill each apple with raisins, sprinkle cinnamon, drizzle honey, put them in your air fryer and cook at 190°C for 18 minutes.
2. Leave them to cool down and serve.

Nutrition: calories 225, fat 4gg, fibre 4g, carbs 6g, protein 10g

Lentils Cookies

Preparation time: 10 minutes
Cooking time: 16 minutes
Servings: 30
Ingredients:

- 120g of white flour
- 100g of brown sugar
- 200g of canned lentils, drained and mashed
- 100g of coconut, unsweetened and shredded
- 1 teaspoon cinnamon powder
- 130g of whole wheat flour
- 50ml of water
- ½ teaspoon nutmeg, ground
- 80g of butter, soft
- 80g of rolled oats
- 120g of white sugar
- 1 egg
- 2 teaspoons almond extract
- 80g of raisins
- 1 teaspoon baking powder

Directions:
1. In a bowl, mix white and whole wheat flour with salt, cinnamon, baking powder and nutmeg and stir.
2. In a bowl, mix butter with white and brown sugar and stir using your kitchen mixer for 2 minutes.
3. Add egg, almond extract, lentils mix, flour mix, oats, raisins, and coconut and stir everything well.
4. Scoop tablespoons of dough on a lined baking sheet that fits your air fryer, introduce them in the fryer and cook at 180°C for 15 minutes.
5. Arrange cookies on a serving platter and serve Enjoy!

Nutrition: calories 150, fat 3g, fibre 2g, carbs 5g, protein 7g

Vanilla Sponge Cake

Preparation time: 10 minutes
Cooking time: 20 minutes
Servings: 10
Ingredients:
- 60g of cornstarch
- 350g of flour
- 15ml of lemon juice
- 2 teaspoons vanilla extract
- 3 teaspoons baking powder
- 250g of sugar
- 1 teaspoon baking soda
- 30ml olive oil
- 50ml of milk
- 2 cups water

Directions:
1. In a bowl, mix flour with cornstarch, baking powder, baking soda and sugar and whisk well.
2. In another bowl, mix oil with milk, water, vanilla and lemon juice and whisk.
3. Combine the two mixtures, stir, pour in a greased baking dish that fits into the tower air fryer, introduce in the fryer and cook at 180°C for 20 minutes.
4. Leave cake to cool down, cut and serve. Enjoy!

Nutrition: calories 240, fat 4g, fibre 1g, carbs 5g, protein 3g

Air Fried Bananas

Preparation time: 10 minutes
Cooking time: 15 minutes
Servings: 5
Ingredients:
- 100g of corn flour
- 3 tablespoons butter
- 150g of panko
- 2 eggs
- 3 tablespoons cinnamon sugar
- 8 bananas, peeled and halved

Directions:
1. Heat up a large pan with the 3 tablespoons of butter over medium high heat, add panko, stir and cook for 4 minutes and then transfer to a bowl.
2. Roll each in flour, eggs and panko mix, arrange them in your air fryer's basket, dust with cinnamon sugar and cook at 150°C for 15 minutes.
3. Serve right away.

Nutrition: calories 160, fat 1g, fibre 5g, carbs 30g, protein 5g

CONCLUSION

The Tower Air Fryer Cookbook is a fantastic resource for those looking to cook amazing and healthy meals using their tower air fryer. The recipes are easy to follow, delicious, and, most importantly, healthy. Whether you are looking for breakfast ideas, poultry recipes, beef and pork dishes, seafood fare, or vegan options, we hope this Tower Air Fryer Cookbook will help you in your journey to healthier eating.

We hope this Tower Air Fryer Cookbook will help you on your journey to healthier eating. With its easy-to-follow recipes and delicious, healthy options, it is a fantastic resource for anyone looking to make better food choices. So what are you waiting for? Get cooking!

Printed in Great Britain
by Amazon

15677963R00045